en. 23/23 £2.50

Fun-to-Know About

Dinosaurs

D1646674

Also in Armada by Michèle Brown

Fun-to-Know About DOGS

Michele Brown

Fun-to-Know About

Dinosaurs

Illustrated by Colin Hawkins and Ellis Nadler

Armada

An Armada Original

Fun-to-Know About Dinosaurs was first
published in the U.K. in Armada in 1978
by Fontana Paperbacks,
14 St. James's Place, London SW1A 1PS

© Michele Brown 1978

Printed in Great Britain by
Love & Malcomson Ltd., Brighton Road,
Redhill, Surrey.

Contents

The World of Dinosaurs

In the Beginning

Hundreds of millions of years ago, life on earth first began in the sea. Creatures that didn't look at all as we would expect living animals to look, but seemed more like plants and flowers and corals and shells, swarmed in the water. Millions of years later, the sea was filled with fish. Millions of years later still, some of those fish came out of the sea and on to the land, and looked less and less like fish as they developed tiny legs. Even more millions of years later, some of those creatures settled on land. They became the first reptiles.

The word reptile comes from the Latin and means 'those who crawl', and reptiles of all sorts have been crawling around the earth now for many millions of years. There are reptiles all over the world to this day: they are cold-blooded and scaly-skinned and they include snakes and lizards, crocodiles and alligators, turtles and tortoises. Once upon a time, the family of reptiles included dinosaurs.

What Were Dinosaurs?

The word dinosaur comes from two Greek words, '*deinos*' and '*saurus*', meaning 'terrible lizard'. Not all dinosaurs were terrible and none of them, in fact, were lizards, but when the name was invented at the beginning of the last century it seemed a suitable one to give these strange prehistoric creatures about which so little was then known.

Far from everything is known about them today, but over the past one hundred and fifty years an enormous amount has been learned – and most of that knowledge has come from the study of fossils. Fossils are any remains of past life that have been preserved in rock or stone. They can be footprints or bones or skeletons or eggs, or even whole animals and plants.

It is by carefully studying the thousands of prehistoric fossils that have been unearthed in the last century and a half that scientists have been able to build up the picture we now have of dinosaurs. Naturally, the picture is far from complete – not least because the soft parts of the dinosaurs almost always rotted away long before they could be fossilised, so that although scientists have learned a lot from fossilised skulls and bones and teeth, they haven't had fossils of muscles and skin tissues and stomachs to examine, and new information is constantly being added as new fossils are discovered. For example, it is possible that there was a dinosaur that was even bigger than Brachiosaurus, the dinosaur that most scientists think is the largest dinosaur to have existed. Fossilised remains of a dinosaur called Titanosaurus have been found and they suggest that he was almost a hundred feet long! Was Titanosaurus even bigger than Brachiosaurus? No one can tell for certain *yet*. One day, more fossils may be discovered that will give scientists the final answer.

Dinosaurs weren't lizards, but they were reptiles of a sort, although the first dinosaurs were totally unlike any reptiles now living. They stood and walked and ran on their hindlegs, whereas the reptiles we know that aren't snakes or legless lizards all crawl about on the four legs that come out of the sides of their bodies. Even the dinosaurs that came millions and millions of years after the first dinosaurs and *did* move on all fours were basically two-legged creatures: their bodies had simply become too big and bulky to be carried on two legs alone, so their front legs evolved to make them four-legged dinosaurs.

Meat-Eating Dinosaurs

The early dinosaurs were small creatures. They were also meat-eaters and they scurried about at speed on their hindlegs, using their short forelegs like arms to catch hold of and tear at their prey. They fed on other small reptiles and even on other smaller dinosaurs.

As millions of years passed, some of these meat-eating dinosaurs grew from being the size of a turkey to being several times the size of an elephant. Coelophysis, one of the first dinosaurs, was only about three feet tall and eight feet long – and half of his length was his tail, because a two-legged dinosaur's ability to balance properly depended on his tail. Tyrannosaurus, one of the last dinosaurs, was about twenty feet tall and about forty-five feet long.

Large or small, the meat-eaters were fierce and hungry hunters. The smaller ones could move at speed, while the larger ones were naturally not so nimble. However, all the meat-eating dinosaurs, whatever their size, stood on their hindlegs. Surprisingly, they were in a minority. Most dinosaurs weren't meat-eaters at all. They were plant-eaters.

Plant-Eating Dinosaurs

Up until a hundred million years ago, the plant-eating dinosaurs fed off the soft plants with which the earth abounded. Later dinosaurs had stronger jaws and teeth and they were able to eat the harder, tougher plants that existed in their time. The last dinosaurs were probably even able to eat the flowering plants that began to appear between seventy and a hundred million years ago.

Many of the smaller plant-eating dinosaurs continued to walk on their hindlegs. Others grew to such an incredible size that they could only support themselves on all fours – and then with difficulty. Brachiosaurus, for example, probably weighed all of fifty tons. It was because of their size that many of the largest dinosaurs spent much of their time in water. The water helped support their massive bodies. They were also safer out in the deep because the meat-eating dinosaurs wouldn't pursue them beyond the shallows.

Anatosaurus

Reptile Hips and Bird Hips

Dinosaurs are divided into two groups according to the structure of their hip bones. These are the *reptile-hipped* dinosaurs and the *bird-hipped* dinosaurs.

The reptile-hipped dinosaurs include:

Carnosaurs – big dinosaurs with great big heads, short necks and massive bones. Their hindlegs were big and their front ones were small. All were meat-eaters and fierce hunters.

Allosaurus

Coelurosaurs – small dinosaurs, almost bird-like, with hollow bones, small heads and long necks.

Ornithosuchus

Sauropods – usually gigantic, four-footed dinosaurs with very heavy bones, small heads and long necks.

Cetiosaurus

The bird-hipped dinosaurs include:

Ornithopods – dinosaurs that usually walked on two legs, with some that could walk on all fours.

Pachycephalosaurus

Stegosaurs – four-footed types with front limbs shorter than the back ones, and bodies protected by armour plating and/or spikes.

Stegosaurus

Ankylosaurs – stocky, armoured types with short legs and broad feet, bony, plated body armour, sometimes with spikes and tails ending in a heavy club.

Nodosaurus

Ceratopsids – mainly four-footed, these came in various sizes but all had large heads, sometimes gigantic and horned.

Triceratops

The most important feature of the dinosaurs was the position of their hind limbs. These rested underneath their bodies, with the elbows directed backwards and the knees forwards – as they are in mammals. With limbs like this, dinosaurs could stand, walk or run with far less effort. Just compare this way of walking to the amphibians or primitive reptiles that rest on their bellies with their legs splayed out on either side.

Were Dinosaurs Hot-Blooded?

Recent evidence suggests that they were, and that they could control their body temperature. Scientists think this because they have cut the fossilised bones of dinosaurs into very thin slices which, under the microscope, show that the bony tissues were riddled with blood vessels, as they are in the bones of mammals, which are the most efficient of all animals when it comes to keeping their body temperature stable. It may also be that the meat-eating dinosaurs ate so much meat because they needed it to make energy to keep their bodies at a stable temperature. Modern warm-blooded meat-eaters like lions and tigers do the same, but cold-blooded killers like crocodiles don't need nearly so much to eat. A three hundred-pound lion eats its own weight of meat every five weeks, and most of this is converted into energy to heat the body. Scientists think that some of the dinosaurs may have done the same.

Male and Female Dinosaurs

Male and female dinosaurs haven't been identified, but we think that there were probably male and female dinosaurs because of differences in body sizes and the shapes and sizes of their crests. Most modern reptiles lay eggs, and scientists believe the dinosaurs did the same, although the only definite fossils of dinosaur eggs come from Protoceratops (and were found in Mongolia).

Dinosaurs didn't just appear on the face of the earth overnight. They evolved over millions and millions of years. It is hard enough trying to imagine a hundred years, let alone a hundred times a hundred times a hundred years, which is what a million years amounts to!

The first dinosaurs appeared about two hundred million years ago. The last dinosaurs disappeared about seventy million years ago. During the one hundred and thirty million years in between, dinosaurs dominated the earth. They were the commonest land animals of their time and they came in all shapes and sizes; some were as large as houses, some were as small as chickens.

The period of time between two hundred and twenty-five and sixty-five million years ago is called the Mesozoic Era – 'the middle era of time'. It is also called the Age of Reptiles, because during these many millions of years, reptiles of all types dominated the land and also the seas. From one ancient reptilian stock, the thecodonts ('socket-toothed'), came the dinosaurs, crocodiles and pterodactyls – and also the birds. It wasn't just a case of one reptile turning into another one, the earth was literally crawling with the creatures and for a lot of this time the dinosaurs existed side by side with reptiles we can recognise today, like snakes, lizards, turtles and crocodiles. There were also curious, mammal-like reptiles with fur, and strange, soft-bodied amphibians.

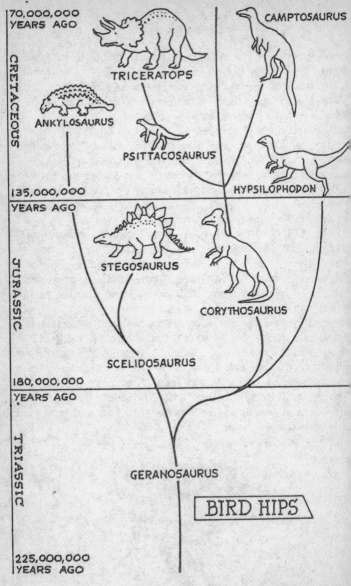

70,000,000
YEARS AGO

CAMPTOSAURUS

TRICERATOPS

ANKYLOSAURUS

PSITTACOSAURUS

HYPSILOPHODON

135,000,000
YEARS AGO

STEGOSAURUS

CORYTHOSAURUS

SCELIDOSAURUS

180,000,000
YEARS AGO

GERANOSAURUS

BIRD HIPS

225,000,000
YEARS AGO

The Ag

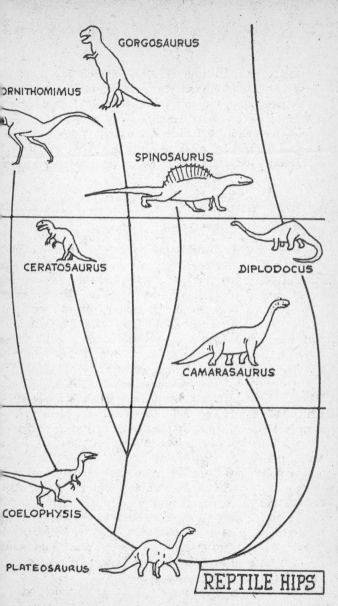

GORGOSAURUS

ORNITHOMIMUS

SPINOSAURUS

CERATOSAURUS

DIPLODOCUS

CAMARASAURUS

COELOPHYSIS

PLATEOSAURUS

REPTILE HIPS

Dinosaurs

The Mesozoic Era is divided into three important periods: See chart on pages 22–23.

The TRIASSIC Period, which lasted from two hundred and twenty-five million years ago to one hundred and eighty million years ago. The JURASSIC Period, which lasted from one hundred and eighty million years ago to one hundred and thirty-five million years ago. The CRETACEOUS Period, which lasted from one hundred and thirty-five million years ago to seventy million years ago.

See chart on pages 22–23.

LIFE IN THE TRIASSIC PERIOD

Imagine a hot, dry world – but not one in which the land masses are arranged as they are today. Two hundred million years ago there was only one huge continent, called Pangea, divided into two parts. The southern part was called Gondwanaland and included South America, Africa, India, the Antarctic and Australia. The northern part was called Laurasia, and was made up of North America, Europe and Asia. Surrounding these land areas was the great ocean of Tethys, which today has shrunk in size and is called the Mediterranean Sea. Although the climate of the time was dry, there were flash floods, and around the coasts and along the river beds, plants, giant ferns and mosses grew. By the second half of the Triassic period, primitive seed plants called cycads had evolved, and primitive pine trees spread beyond the river banks on to the uplands. The oldest remains of dinosaurs of this time come from South America and southern Africa, but because all the continents were joined together they must have roamed freely all over the land. During the Triassic period there were small mammals, huge crocodiles and great lumbering tortoises, while in the seas there were fish with soft fin rays. During the Upper Triassic period, the lightly-built coelurosaurs existed side by side with the first of the 'heavies', the great plant-eating sauropods.

Brachiosaurus

LIFE IN THE JURASSIC PERIOD

Between one hundred and ninety and one hundred and forty million years ago, things had changed: the climate was wetter and warmer, and vast swamps covered much of the land. Maidenhair trees and conifers were the dominant plants. North America drifted from Gondwanaland. The seas were warm and clear, with huge lagoons – one lagoon stretched over a thousand miles across Portugal through France to Southern Germany. Coral reefs fringed the shores, sharks hunted colourful fish and

pterodactyls flew in the skies. But what of the dinosaurs? Well, they lived both in the swamps and in what remained of the dry desert areas. There were large sauropods and carnosaurs and medium-sized camptosaurs and coelurosaurs. Many new types evolved during this period. Herds of plant-eating dinosaurs were hunted by the fierce meat-eaters, while the smaller dinosaurs had a variety of vegetation and small animals to feed on. Crocodiles, turtles and lizards increased in numbers and, in many cases, adapted to life in the seas.

LIFE IN THE CRETACEOUS PERIOD

In the Cretaceous period, the positions of the continents were still very different from what they are today, but they were beginning to take their modern shape. India split off from Australia and Antarctica, while the island of Madagascar broke away from mainland Africa. Most of the earth was flat, the climate was warm and the seas were clear. Flowering plants appeared in greater numbers and forms, especially in the northern hemisphere where there were oak and pine forests, giant redwoods, monkey puzzle trees and magnolias. By the end of the Cretaceous period there were sycamores, figs, maples and palms, and insects took nectar from these plants and in their turn pollenated each flower.

The bird-hipped dinosaurs were dominant, and in the northern hemisphere they evolved into a variety of forms. Most of our dinosaur records for this period come from north-western North America and eastern Asia. In North America, the duck-billed dinosaurs, hadrosaurs, roamed the forests in herds and were the main herbivores of the time. It seems that the armoured ankylosaurs preferred more open country, while the dome-headed dinosaurs lived in groups on higher land. Gorgosaurus was the dominant carnosaur, and small coelurosaurs existed on a diet of small lizards, snakes and small mammals.

By the end of the Cretaceous period, the hadrosaurs had declined and the ceratopsians took over as the main plant-eaters. These formidable animals were protected by a huge collar and horns, and it needed a very powerful beast to deal with such prey – so Tyrannosaurus evolved as a killer of gigantic proportions, one of the last dinosaurs to roam the earth.

The End of the Dinosaurs

About seventy million years ago, having dominated the animal kingdom for a hundred and thirty million years or so, the dinosaurs disappeared. Plant-eaters and flesh-eaters became extinct. Why?

The honest answer is that nobody knows for sure. There are several possible explanations. For one, the wonderfully warm climate that the cold-blooded dinosaurs enjoyed began to change. Seventy million years ago the world was becoming a cooler place. The warm swamp-lands were drying up. The plant-life was changing: the stems, branches and leaves were getting tougher. It is possible that the dinosaurs couldn't adapt to the changes. The plant-eaters couldn't get used to the tougher plants and so died out. The meat-eaters no longer had the plant-eaters to feed on.

Another possible explanation is that seventy million years ago some terrible disaster affected the dinosaurs. They may have been killed by a dinosaur disease that swept the world.

All the same, it is curious that while some reptiles were able to adapt to the changing climate and were able to survive the ravages of nature and time, the dinosaurs were not. Their era came to a very definite end seventy million years ago. The age of the dinosaur was over. The age of the mammal began.

Dinosaur Discoveries

Almost everything that is known about dinosaurs and other prehistoric animals has been learned from studying fossils and the rocks in which they have been found. Although people have been collecting fossils for a thousand years or more, it is only within the last two hundred years that the study of fossils has become a serious science and that palaeontologists – people who study fossils – have realised that fossils can teach us an enormous amount about life on earth millions of years ago.

The first recorded discovery of a dinosaur was mentioned by the Reverend Robert Plot in his *Natural History of Oxfordshire* in 1677. In a quarry in Cornwall he found the lower part of a gigantic thigh bone. He didn't know it was from a dinosaur and thought it belonged to some giant human being. It is lucky that he made a drawing of it, because the original bone has been lost. From his drawing we think the bone belonged to the big meat-eating dinosaur Megalosaurus.

It wasn't until 1824 and 1825 that two dinosaurs were recognised as dinosaurs and given names: the first was Megalosaurus, the second was Iguanodon. In the hundred and fifty years since then, thousands of specimens of the fossilised remains of hundreds of different types of dinosaurs have been discovered all over the world. The map on pages 30 and 31 will show you where some of the most famous dinosaur discoveries have been made.

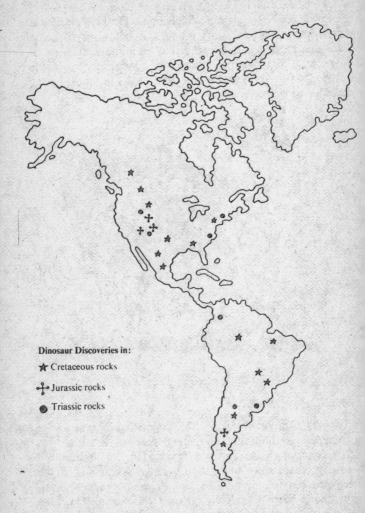

Dinosaur Discoveries in:

★ Cretaceous rocks

✝ Jurassic rocks

● Triassic rocks

The British have been pioneers among dinosaur discoverers and many of the most interesting specimens of prehistoric life have been found in Britain. Iguanodon was discovered by an English couple called Gideon and Mary Mantell. Another Englishwoman who lived at the beginning of the nineteenth century, Mary Anning, found the first pterodactyl to be discovered in England. Sir Richard Owen, who was born in 1804, was the man who gave the group of reptiles the collective name of 'dinosaurs'.

Probably the most famous dinosaur discovery in Europe was made by Louis Dollo, who studied the skeletons of thirty-one Iguanodons found in a coal mine in Belgium in 1878. Several of the most famous dinosaur discoveries have been made in western North America, particularly in the state of Utah where there are soft clays, shales and sandstone dating from the Upper Jurassic period, and Hell Creek in Montana, where light-coloured sandstone rocks have given us the remains of the last dinosaurs, those that lived in the Upper Cretaceous period, only seventy million years ago!

In the 1890's, dinosaur hunters in covered wagons struck out across North America and spent many dusty days and rough nights at sites like Camo Buff and Bone Cabin Quarry in Wyoming. Today in the American state of Colorado there is even a town called Dinosaur, with street names like Tyrannosaurus Terrace and Brontosaurus Boulevard!

Dinosaur Dictionary

In this Dinosaur Dictionary you will find listed many of the best-known and most important dinosaurs. There were, of course, hundreds of others that haven't been included. We know something about some of the ones that haven't been listed here – Teratosaurus, Torosaurus and Trilophosaurus, for example – but there must have been scores of dinosaurs about whom we know absolutely nothing.

The descriptions and pictures of the dinosaurs in this Dictionary have been drawn from what scientists have discovered in the past one hundred and fifty years. They can be certain about some things, but not at all sure about others. A lot of the 'facts' about dinosaurs are really the result of intelligent guess-work. No one has ever seen a live dinosaur and no scientist has been able to examine the actual body of a dead dinosaur. Nobody will ever be able to know what colour they were. But from what is known and from what has been discovered, a vivid picture emerges, and it is that picture you will see in the pages that follow.

Acanthopholis

Acanthopholis was a plant-eating dinosaur with a wonderfully protective coat of armour covering it. It wasn't very big, but its body was a mass of bony knobs and spikes and lumps and bumps that must have helped it survive many an encounter with a hungry meat-eater.

Pronounciation. Ah-kan-THOFF-olis
Name. 'Prickly scaled lizard'
Type. Primitive ankylosaur
Period. Lower Cretaceous (135–100 million years ago)
Measurements. 3 metres (10 feet) long, 1 metre (3 feet) high
Food. Plants
Where found. Europe

Allosaurus

Allosaurus was one of the largest and fiercest of all dinosaurs. It was a giant: at least ten metres from the front of its massive jaw to the tip of its huge tail. It was with the aid of this muscular tail that it kept its balance as it stood and walked and ran on its two very big and immensely powerful hindlegs.

It had an enormous head, with a jaw like a crocodile's and an impressive set of sharp, ferocious fangs. Almost the smallest things about it were its arms: but what they lacked in size was well made up for by the sharpness of its claws. It had strong, curved claws as well on the three giant toes on its hind feet. It used its claws and jaws to devastating effect because Allosaurus was a savage meat-eater. It had a tremendous appetite and the might to satisfy it. It probably hunted big sauropods like Apatosaurus and plated dinosaurs like Stegosaurus.

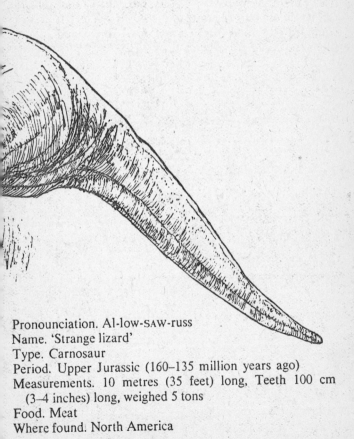

Pronounciation. Al-low-SAW-russ
Name. 'Strange lizard'
Type. Carnosaur
Period. Upper Jurassic (160–135 million years ago)
Measurements. 10 metres (35 feet) long, Teeth 100 cm (3–4 inches) long, weighed 5 tons
Food. Meat
Where found. North America

Anatosaurus

Anatosaurus had a huge body and, on land, usually walked on its two hefty hindlegs, although it could drop down on to all fours. Its front feet were webbed and it used them and its powerful tail for swimming.

It was a plant-eater and used its broad, flat jaw, that looked like a huge duck's bill, to dig out food from the ground and the water's bed. Like most of the other plant-eating dinosaurs, Anatosaurus was no fighter. It wasn't equipped to hunt – its claws were small and blunt.

Although its skin was tough, it had no protective armour-plating. In fact, its only place of refuge was the water and, when pursued by a hungry meat-eater, the only way to reach safety was to plunge into deep water and stay there.

Pronounciation. Ah-nat-toe-SAW-russ
Name. 'Duck lizard'
Type. Hadrosaur
Period. Upper Cretaceous (80 million years ago)
Measurements. 9 metres (30 feet) long, 3.5 metres (12 feet) high, weighed several tons
Food. Plants, probably pine needles and twigs
Where found. North America

Apatosaurus

Apatosaurus is commonly, but incorrectly, called Bronto-saurus. It was a gentle giant, a plant-eater who was safer and more comfortable in water than on land.

It had a huge, long, tapering tail, a great body, four enormous legs like stocky pillars, a thick long neck and then a comparatively tiny head with a small mouth that contained two dozen very feeble teeth. Given its great size, its great weight and its small mouth, it is not surprising that it was no match for hungry meat-eaters like Allosaurus. It did what it could to fend off the enemy with its long, strong tail, but faced with really sharp claws and jaws there was nothing it could do.

Pronounciation. Ah-pat-oe-SAW-russ
Name. 'Unreal lizard'
Type. Sauropod
Period. Upper Triassic (190 million years ago)
Measurements. 21 metres (70 feet) long, weighed over 30 tons
Food. Soft water plants
Where found. North America

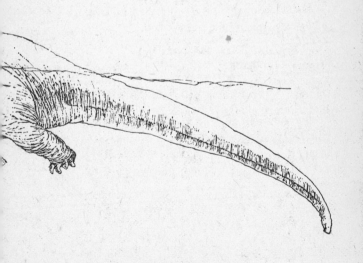

Brachiosaurus

Brachiosaurus is the dinosaur with the biggest body and one of the smallest brains. Its whole frame weighed about fifty tons while its whole brain weighed only a few ounces. Brachiosaurus means 'arm lizard' in Greek and it was given this name because, unlike most dinosaurs, it had huge forearms. They were really front legs, although longer and even heavier than its already massive rear legs.

Brachiosaurus was not only simple, it was also slow. On land it moved about with great difficulty at a top speed of 2 m.p.h. and was an easy prey for a hungry meat-eater. Brachiosaurus was too clumsy and slow to escape from an enemy, so it sought refuge in the safety of the water. It could also stay under cover in the water thanks to the fact that its nostrils were placed in a dome right on top of its head, so that it could breathe with just the very top of its head showing above the water. It couldn't swim, so never went out of its depth, but its long neck enabled it to pick plants off the water's bed.

Pronounciation. Brack-ee-oh-SAW-russ
Name. 'Arm lizard'
Type. Sauropod
Period. Upper Jurassic (160–135 million years ago)
Measurements. 30 metres (85 feet) long, head held
    12 metres (40 feet) above ground, weighed 50 tons
Food. Soft water plants
Where found. North America and East Africa

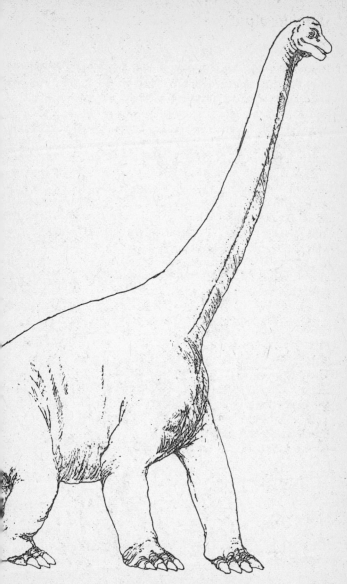

Camarasaurus

Camarasaurus was a cousin of the gigantic Apatosaurus. It was a plant-eater who walked on all fours, and had peg-like teeth along the edges of its jaws.

Pronounciation. Kam-uh-rah-SAW-russ
Name. 'Arched chamber lizard'
Type. Sauropod
Period. Upper Jurassic (160–135 million years ago)
Measurements. 10.5 metres (35 feet) long
Food. Plants
Where found. North America

Camptosaurus

Camptosaurus is Greek for 'bent lizard' and this dinosaur got its name because it could bend down and walk on all fours as well as being able to stand and walk on its two hindlegs. It had an unusual face even for a dinosaur, with a horny beak at the front of its mouth and a set of not-very-good teeth at the back of its jaw.

Camptosaurus was another plant-eater. It used its beak for pecking at the plants it wanted to eat and then chewed the plants with the teeth at the back of its jaw. It had no protective armour and its means of self-defence were few, so it was another of the plant-eaters who fell easy prey to the brutal meat-eating dinosaurs.

Pronounciation. Kam-toe-SAW-russ
Name. 'Bent lizard'
Type. Ornithopod
Period. Upper Jurassic (160–135 million years ago)
Measurements. 5 metres (16 feet) long, weighed over 3 tons
Food. Plants
Where found. North America

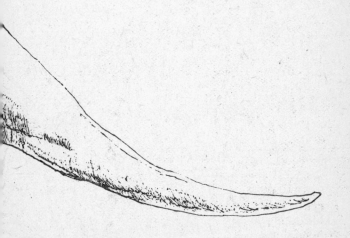

Ceratosaurus

Ceratosaurus was one of the fiercest of the meat-eating dinosaurs. It walked on huge hind legs and had a large bony horn on its nose making it a very recognisable and unpleasant-looking monster. At the ends of its short arms were four-fingered hands with sharp claws at the end of each finger and inside its big mouth were a fine set of razor-sharp teeth.

Pronounciation. Seh-rat-oh-SAW-russ
Name. 'Horned lizard'
Type. Carnosaur
Period. Jurassic (150 million years ago)
Measurements. 5 metres (16 feet) long
Food. Meat
Where found. North America

Cetiosaurus

Most of the remains of the giant sauropods come from North America, but some skeletons have been found in Britain. Cetiosaurus with vast body, heavy bones and heavy feet, is one.

Pronounciation. Seh-tee-oh-SAW-russ
Name. 'Whale lizard'
Type. Sauropod
Period. Jurassic (160 million years ago)
Measurements. 15 metres (50 feet) long
Food. Plants
Where found. Central England

Chasmosaurus

Chasmosaurus was a harmless, plant-eating dinosaur roughly the size of an elephant. It looked not unlike its much more famous cousin, Triceratops. It had a massive head and out of the back of it grew a collar of bone that protected its neck and shoulders. It had a short, sharp horn above each eye and a third short horn on its nose.

Pronounciation. Kaz-mo-SAW-russ
Name. 'Gaping lizard'
Type. Ceratopsian
Period. Upper Cretaceous (70 million years ago)
Measurements. 4.5–6 metres (15–20 feet) long
Food. Plants
Where found. North America and Mongolia

Chialingosaurus

Chialingosaurus walked on all fours, although its forelegs were much smaller than its hefty hindlegs. Its main source of protection from attack by meat-eaters were two overlapping rows of heavy bone plates that stood out on its back and stretched from behind its head to the tip of its tail where it had four sharp spikes.

Pronounciation. Key-ah-ling-oh-SAW-russ
Name. Named after the place where the fossil was found in China
Type. Stegosaur
Period. Upper Jurassic (150 million years ago)
Measurements. 6 metres (20 feet) long
Food. Plants
Where found. Eastern Asia

Coelophysis

Coelophysis was one of the first of all the dinosaurs. It wasn't enormous – none of the earliest dinosaurs were – but it was fierce and, being a meat-eater, there were few other creatures at the time who were safe from it. It may even have hunted fellow specimens of Coelophysis.

It stood on its two bird-like hindlegs and when on the move, with his long neck stretched forward and its even longer tail stretched behind, it was no more than two feet in height.

It had small forearms with little four-fingered hands, on which three of the fingers had nasty, sharp claws, and each of its feet had three sharp-clawed toes. Inside its sizeable lizard-like mouth were a set of small, incredibly sharp teeth and it used these to tear out the hunks of meat from the bodies of its prey. It could move at speed on its thin legs and had little difficulty pouncing on the other creatures who travelled less swiftly and on all fours.

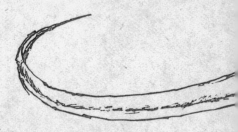

Pronounciation. See-low-FY-siss
Name. 'Hollow form'
Type. Coelurosaur
Period. Upper Triassic (180 million years ago)
Measurements. 2.5–3 metres (8–10 feet) long, weighed 18–23 kilogrammes (40–50 pounds)
Food. Meat
Where found. North America

Compsognathus

Compsognathus was the tiniest of all known dinosaurs. It was only the size of a modern chicken, though its appearance was as strange as you would expect a prehistoric monster's to be.

It had a long thin neck, an even longer tail and it was able to run at speed on its two hind legs. It was a meat eater prepared to eat almost any creature that was small enough and weak enough to be its prey. It caught and ate creatures such as prehistoric insects and lizards and turtles. It even fed on dead fish and shell-fish that it found washed up on the shore.

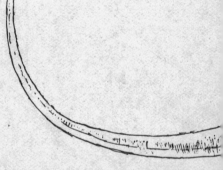

Because of a recently-discovered fossil skeleton of Compsognathus found in West Germany, some scientists believe that this dinosaur, unlike most other dinosaurs, gave birth to its young in the same way as modern mammals do. Inside the fossil skeleton was another, much smaller fossil skeleton positioned just where the Compsognathus' stomach would have been. It is possible that the tiny skeleton was that of a baby Compsognathus growing inside its mother.

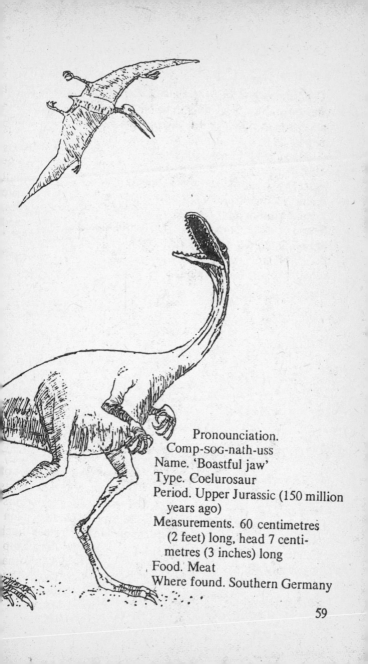

Pronounciation.
Comp-sog-nath-uss
Name. 'Boastful jaw'
Type. Coelurosaur
Period. Upper Jurassic (150 million
    years ago)
Measurements. 60 centimetres
    (2 feet) long, head 7 centi-
    metres (3 inches) long
Food. Meat
Where found. Southern Germany

59

Corythosaurus

Corythosaurus was a duck-billed plant-eating dinosaur who spent a lot of its time in water. In size and appearance it resembled Anatosaurus, except that it had a large and striking crest of bone on top of its head that may have helped increase its sense of smell.

Pronounciation. Kor-ith-oh-SAW-russ
Name. 'Helmet lizard'
Type. Ornithopod
Period. Upper Cretaceous (76–70 million years ago)
Measurements. 9 metres (30 feet) long
Food. Plants
Where found. North America

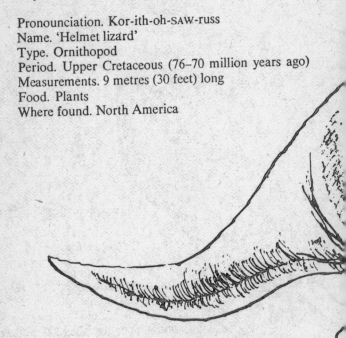

Diplodocus

The name Diplodocus means 'double beam' and it had an immensely long neck and an immensely long tail to match. Walking on land it would use one to balance the other. Its body was big, too, and it moved about very slowly on four big legs. It was the longest of all the dinosaurs.

It had a tiny brain and a mouth that was almost as small. To get enough food through that minute, weak-toothed mouth to be able to sustain that giant body, Diplodocus must have had to spend all its time eating. Certainly it didn't waste any time moving about unnecessarily. It stayed as much as possible in the safety of the water. It had eyes and nostrils right on top of its small head which enabled it to see and breathe with only the top of its head showing above the surface of the water and it had a very long neck which enabled it to reach down to pick up the vegetation it needed as its food for survival.

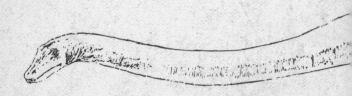

Pronounciation. Dee-PLOD-oh-kuss
Name. 'Double beam'
Type. Sauropod
Period. Upper Jurassic (150 million years ago)
Measurements. 26.5 metres (87 feet) long
Food. Soft plants
Where found. North America

Euoplocephalus

Euoplocephalus was a plant-eating dinosaur with a strong protective covering of armour. All over its body it had large pointed knobs and on the tip of its tail was a mighty knob of bone covered in ridges that must have been a powerful weapon.

Pronounciation. You-oh-SEF-ah-luss
Name. 'Well-protected head'
Type. Ankylosaur
Period. Upper Cretaceous (100–70 million years ago)
Measurements. Over 5 metres (16 feet) long
Food. Plants
Where found. North America

Gorgosaurus

Gorgosaurus was one of the mighty descendants of Allo-saurus, and with its massive body, heavy tail, strong hind-legs and sharply-taloned, three-toed feet, it looked rather like its fierce ancestor – though Gorgosaurus was even bigger than Allosaurus.

Pronounciation. Gore-go-SAW russ
Name. 'Monster lizard'
Type. Carnosaur
Period. Upper Cretaceous (90 million years ago)
Measurements. Over 12 metres (40 feet) long, 4.5 metres (15 feet) high
Food. Meat
Where found. North America and eastern Asia

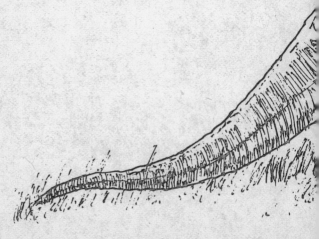

Hypsilophodon

The tiny Hypsilophodon looked very much like a miniature Iguanodon. It was one of the smallest of all dinosaurs, being the size of an average turkey, with a thick neck, a large body (for its overall size) and quite a long tail. It walked and ran on its hindlegs and was a peace-loving plant-eater.

Pronounciation. Hip-see-LOAF-oh-don
Name. 'High ridged tooth'
Type. Ornithopod
Period. Lower Cretaceous (115 million years ago)
Measurements. 1.5–2 metres (5–6 feet) long, 50 centimetres
    (2 feet) high, weighed 63 kilogrammes (140 pounds)
Food. Plants
Where found. Isle of Wight, England

Iguanodon

Iguanodon was the second dinosaur to be named and described in modern times. In 1825, when some of its huge teeth were found, it was thought they resembled the teeth of an iguana, although, of course, much, much larger, which is how Iguanodon got its name. (In fact, the iguana is in no way related to Iguanodon.)

Iguanodon was a descendant of Camptosaurus. It had rather unusual webbed feet, which made it easier for it to walk over soft, wet ground, and well-developed hands that featured a most unusual sharp spike where you would expect the thumb to be. Being a plant-eater it may even have used these hands to hold its food.

In parts of southern England the remains of Iguanodon are quite common and a number of Iguanodon skeletons have been found together. This suggests the possibility that at some point whole herds of Iguanodon died together as a result of a natural disaster.

Pronounciation. Ee-GWA-no-don
Name. 'Iguana tooth'
Type. Ornithopod
Period. Lower Cretaceous (136–115 million years ago)
Measurements. Over 9 metres (30 feet) long, 5 metres (16 feet) high, weighed 4–5 tons
Food. Plants
Where found. Southern England, Belgium, North Africa and Spitzbergen in the Arctic

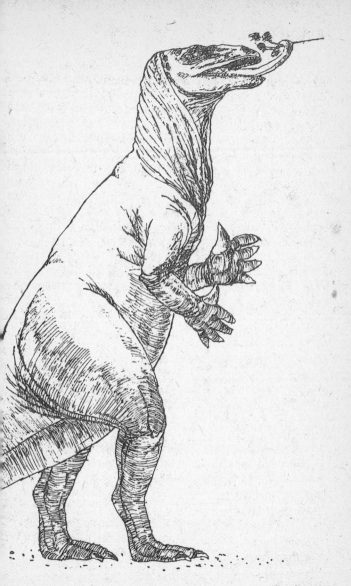

Kentrosaurus

Kentrosaurus was a cousin of Stegosaurus and Chialingosaurus, those two well-covered plant-eating dinosaurs. I wasn't as big as them, and running down its back, from the rear of its head to the tip of its tail, it had rather fewer of the sticking-out plates of bone. However, at the end of its tail it had more than four spikes and it was a powerful tail that must have provided it with a useful means of self protection.

Pronounciation. Ken-tro-SAW-russ
Name. 'Prickly lizard'
Type. Stegosaur
Period. Upper Jurassic (150 million years ago)
Measurements. Over 5 metres (16 feet) long, weighed 1 ton
Food. Soft plants
Where found. East Africa

Kritosaurus

Kritosaurus was one of the ancestors of the plant-eating duck-billed dinosaur, Anatosaurus. Their big bodies looked similar, but their heads were totally unalike. Kritosaurus had a curious bony hump on its nose giving it a face rather like a parrot.

Pronounciation. Cry-toe-SAW-russ
Type. Ornithopod
Period. Upper Cretaceous (76–70 million years ago)
Measurements. 7–8 metres (25–27 feet) long
Food. Plants
Where found. North America

Lambeosaurus

Lambeosaurus was a member of that same family of duck-billed plant-eating dinosaurs that included Anatosaurus, Corythosaurus and Kritosaurus. Its body was much like theirs, but on top of its head was a huge crest that looked like an oddly-shaped hatchet. The crest contained hollow bones which held air and probably enabled it to stay under water longer, either to feed or to hide from ravaging meat-eaters

Pronounciation. Lam-bee-oh-SAW russ
Name. After the palaentologist Lambe
Type. Ornithopod
Period. Upper Cretaceous (76–70 million years ago)
Measurements. 8 metres (26 feet) long
Food. Plants
Where found. North America

Megalosaurus

The name Megalosaurus comes from the Greek meaning 'large lizard' and although it was a fairly big dinosaur it was by no means as enormous as some of the other prehistoric monsters. However, its name may be explained by the fact that it was the very first dinosaur to be given a name, back in 1824.

Pronounciation. Meg-uh-low-SAW-russ
Name. 'Large lizard'
Type. Carnosaur
Period. Jurassic (190–140 million years ago)
Measurements. 6–7 metres (20–23 feet) long, 4 metres (13 feet) high, weighed over 2 tons
Food. Meat
Where found. England and France

Monoclonius

Monoclonius, who was about the size of an elephant although it looked more like a rhinoceros, belonged to the family that included Triceratops. It was a plant-eater who moved on four feet and had a great curved collar of bone growing out of the back of its head. As extra protection it also had a couple of small horns growing above its eyes and one enormous, sharp horn growing out of its nose.

Pronounciation. MON-oh-KLO-nee-uss
Name. 'Single horn'
Type. Ceratopsid
Period. Upper Cretaceous (70 million years ago)
Measurements. 6 metres (20 feet) long
Food. Plants
Where found. North America

Nodosaurus

Nodosaurus was an armoured plant-eating dinosaur whose body was covered with circular lumps of hard bone that acted as a strong protective outer shell.

Pronounciation. Node-oh-SAW-russ
Name. 'Knobbed lizard'
Type. Ankylosaur
Period. Upper Cretaceous (100–70 million years ago)
Measurements. Over 4.5 metres (15 feet) long
Food. Plants
Where found. North America

Ornitholestes

The name Ornitholestes means 'bird stealer' and, naturally enough, the reason scientists gave this meat-eating dinosaur such a name is because they believed that it hunted and trapped birds. It was a small dinosaur, but had long hind-legs and two-pronged feet and could run at speed. On its forelegs it had long, sharp fingers and probably used them to catch and hold its prey.

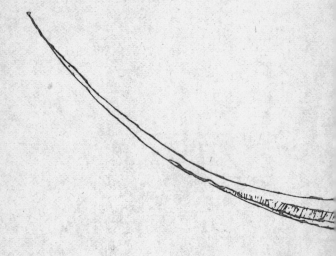

Pronounciation. Awn-ith-oh-LESS-teez
Name. 'Bird stealer'
Type. Coelosaur
Period. Upper Jurassic (150 million years ago)
Measurements. 1.5–2 metres (5–6 feet) long
Food. Meat
Where found. North America

Ornithomimus

Ornithomimus had a long, goose-like neck and an even longer, reptilian tail. It had two long, thin hindlegs on which it walked and ran (at considerable speed, if it chose) and spindly forearms rather like a human being's. It had three fingers on each hand and one of these fingers could grip against the other two.

Ornithomimus was a meat-eater which fed on small prehistoric insects and worms and lizards and which also probably ate eggs – both dinosaur eggs and, when it could get them, bird's eggs. It may well have used its hands to grip the eggs and then have broken into them with its duck-like bill. It had a powerful beak, but no teeth, which was unusual (and a little inconvenient) for a meat-eating dinosaur.

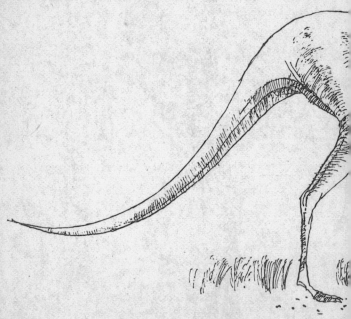

Some scientists believe that Ornithomimus may have been a plant-eater as well as a meat-eater and that it may have used its fingers to get hold of the branches of trees and then eat the leaves and buds growing on them. Other scientists feel that its beak wouldn't have been strong enough to tear up plants: they believe that it only ate other small creatures and the contents of eggs and swallowed them whole.

Pronounciation. Awn-ith-oh-MY-muss
Name. 'Bird imitator'
Type. Coelurosaur
Period. Upper Cretaceous (120–70 million years ago)
Measurements. 3–4 metres (11–14 feet) long
Food. Meat, insects, eggs, fruit
Where found. North America and eastern Asia

Ornithosuchus

Ornithosuchus could run at speed which made it an excellent hunter. It had strong jaws, sharp teeth, and its prey were smaller plant-eating dinosaurs and the young of larger dinosaurs, both meat-eaters and plant-eaters.

Pronounciation. Awn-ith-oh-SUCK-uss
Name. 'Bird crocodile'
Type. Theocodont reptile
Period Upper Triassic (200–195 million years ago)
Measurements. 3 metres (10 feet) long, 1 metre (3 feet) high
Food. Meat
Where found. Scotland

Pachycephalosaurus

Pachycephalosaurus was a plant-eating descendant of the famous Iguanodon but had an extraordinary head on which the dome was made of bone over 2 metres thick! The rest of the head was unusual too, being all covered in lumps and bumps and bits of pointed bone.

Pronounciation. Pak-ee-sef-ah-low-SAW-russ
Name. 'Thick-headed lizard'
Type. Ornithopod
Period. Upper Cretaceous (100–70 million years ago)
Measurements. 6 metres (20 feet) long, dome of skull over 200 centimetres (8 inches) thick
Food. Plants
Where found. North America, Europe, eastern Asia

Paleoscincus

Paleoscincus's armour consisted of rectangular plates of bone covering its back and reaching right down to its tail. Along its sides were rows of big, sharp spikes, not unlike the spikes on the sides of Ankylosaurus, although Paleoscincus didn't have the added protection of a club at the end of its tail.

Pronounciation. Pal-ee-oh-SKINK-uss
Name. 'Ancient kind of lizard'
Type. Ankylosaur
Period. Upper Cretaceous (80–70 million years ago)
Measurements. 4.5 metres (15 feet) long
Food. Plants
Where found. North America

Parasaurolophus

Parasaurolophus was a duck-billed plant-eating dinosaur from the same family as Anatosaurus, Corythosaurus, Kritosaurus and Lambeosaurus, though with a very individual head, the chief feature of which was the large tube of hollow bone that grew out of the back of it and looked like a giant horn. It was able to fill it with air and stay under water.

Pronounciation. Pah-ruh-saw-RAWL-uh-fuss
Name. 'Abnormal crested lizard'
Type. Ornithopod
Period. Upper Cretaceous (100–70 million years ago)
Measurements. 8.5–9.5 metres (28–31 feet) long, crests over 1.5 metres (5 feet) long
Food. Tough plant material
Where found. North America

Pinacosaurus

Pinacosaurus was covered with strong, sharp spikes. They pointed up out of its back, its sides, its legs and its tail, which ended with a large, flat plate of bone with sharp edges that looked more like a battle-axe than a club.

Pronounciation. Pin-ak-oh-SAW-russ
Name. 'Pointed lizard'
Type. Ankylosaur
Period. Upper Cretaceous (100–70 million years ago)
Measurements. 3.5–4.5 metres (12–15 feet) long
Food. Plants
Where found. Eastern Asia

Plateosaurus

The name Plateosaurus means 'flat lizard', but Plateosaurus didn't look flat at all. For a dinosaur of its time it was a big creature, the giant of its generation. It ran on strong hindlegs, but could stand and rest on its small forearms as well.

Pronounciation. Plat-ee-oh-SAW-russ
Name. 'Flat lizard'
Type. Saurischian (early dinosaur)
Period. Upper Triassic (200 million years ago)
Measurements. 6 metres (20 feet) long
Food. Soft plants
Where found. Southern Germany

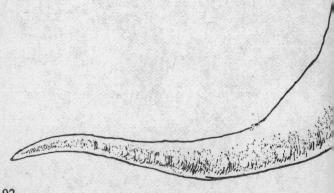

Polacanthus

Polacanthus was a relatively small plant-eating dinosaur
with wonderful armour-plated hide. All down its back
from the rear of its head to its hips, it had two rows of
huge sharp horns. Its hips were covered by a substantial
shield of bone and then a double row of flat, pointed plates
of bone stretched down to the tip of its powerful tail.

Pronounciation. Pole-uh-CAN-thuss
Name. 'Many spined'
Type. Ankylosaur
Period. Lower Cretaceous (over 120 million years ago)
Measurements. 4 metres (14 feet) long, weighed between
    1–2 tons
Food. Soft plants
Where found. Isle of Wight, England

Protoceratops

Protoceratops is a name that comes from three Greek words meaning 'first horned face'. It's an odd name to have chosen for a dinosaur which doesn't appear to have any horns on its face, but the explanation is that Protoceratops was the first in a line of dinosaurs which *did* have horns on their faces.

It was a comparatively small, plant-eating dinosaur, which walked close to the ground on four short legs. It had a body rather like a giant lizard's, with a huge head and a bony beak that looked a little like a parrot's. Coming out of the back of its skull was a large collar of bone that covered the back of its neck and shoulders.

Protoceratops is famous because in 1923, only a year after the first fossil of a Protoceratops skull had been discovered, scientists working in the Gobi desert of Mongolia found their first-ever dinosaur egg and it was a Protoceratops egg. It had been assumed that baby dinosaurs were

hatched from eggs, as is the case with most reptiles, but here was hard proof. The female Protoceratops had laid her eggs, about twenty of them, in the hollow of a sand dune and then covered them over with a loose bed of sand and gone away. The warmth of the sun on the sand would help to hatch the eggs and eventually the baby Protoceratops would break out of its small shell (not much larger than an orange) and make its way into the prehistoric world.

Pronounciation. Pro-toe-SERR-uh-tops
Name. 'First horned face'
Type. Ornithopod
Period. Upper Cretaceous (100–70 million years ago)
Measurements. 2 metres (6 feet) long
Food. Plants
Where found. Eastern Asia

Psittacosaurus

The tongue-twisting name of this dinosaur means 'parrot lizard' and from its picture you will understand why. It was a small meat-eating dinosaur, noted for the sharp, pointed bone on the front of its face which made it look as though it was wearing a parrot's beak.

Pronounciation. Sit-ack-oh-SAW-russ
Name. 'Parrot lizard'
Type. Ornithopod
Period. Lower Cretaceous (110 million years ago)
Measurements. Over 2 metres (6 feet) long
Food. Plants
Where found. Eastern Asia

Spinosaurus

Spinosaurus was a savage meat-eating dinosaur which looked rather like Tyrannosaurus, but on its back it had a giant fin that stood out about two metres and may have been used as a heat regulator as Spinosaurus lived in a hot, subtropical climate.

Pronunciation. Spy-no-SAW-russ
Name. 'Spine lizard'
Type. Carnosaur
Period. Lower Cretaceous (130–100 million years ago)
Measurements. 10.5 metres (35 feet) long, spines on back up to 2 metres (6 feet) long
Food. Meat
Where found. Egypt

Stegosaurus

Stegosaurus's name means 'cover lizard' and there is no doubt that the back of this creature was very well covered. Stretching from just behind its head to almost the tip of its tail were two rows of very heavy bone plating. The bone plates stood out from the back and overlapped one another, but they only acted as armoured protection from attack from above. Its sides were exposed and vulnerable to attack from meat-eaters.

As well as the bone-plating on its back, Stegosaurus did have another means of self-defence in its tail, which had four very sharp, hard spikes, at least two feet long, sticking out of it. Stegosaurus walked on all fours, although it had very short front legs and long, strong hindlegs.

Despite its frightening appearance it was another of the gentle plant-eaters who had armour for protection rather than attack. It was also another of the dim dinosaurs: in its small head was a minute brain (the size of a conker) that controlled its mouth and front legs. Its hindlegs and its tail were controlled by a 'second brain'. It was larger than its actual brain (more the size of a melon) and it was located behind its hips.

Pronounciation. Steg-oh-SAW-russ
Name. 'Cover lizard'
Type. Stegosaur
Period. Upper Jurassic (over 140 million years ago)
Measurements. 9 metres (30 feet) long, spikes on tail 50 centimetres (2 feet) long
Food. Soft plants
Where found. North America and England

Styracosaurus

The spikes on Styracosaurus's face were the most notice-able feature of this plant-eating dinosaur who was almost as big as an elephant but looked more like a rhinoceros. On top of its parrot-beaked nose it had a large, long sharp horn and coming out of the collar of bone that grew out of the back of its head and protected its neck and shoulders were six huge, pointed spikes. It may have been able to charge at its enemies at speeds of up to 30 m.p.h.

Pronounciation. Stih-rack-oh-SAW-russ
Name. 'Spike lizard'
Type. Ceratopsian
Period. Upper Cretaceous (76–70 million years ago)
Measurements. 6 metres (20 feet) long, nose spike measured
    4.5 centimetres (1½ feet)
Food. Plants
Where found. North America

Triceratops

'Three-horned face' is the meaning of the name Triceratops. It had two very sharp horns, about three feet long,
one above each eye, and a third, much shorter, thicker
horn sticking up from its nose. Growing out of the back
of its head was a great collar of bone.

By the standards of dinosaurs it wasn't a giant. Roughly
the size of a large elephant, it had broad feet and toes
with blunt claws, and stocky trunk-like legs to support its
bulky body. It was a plant-eater, but not nearly as peace-
loving as many of the other plant-eating dinosaurs. Judging
from the scars found on the fossils of Triceratops, it is
possible that one male Triceratops would do battle with
another male Triceratops rather as wild deer do today.
The real enemy of Triceratops was Tyrannosaurus, the
mighty meat-eating dinosaur. When they fought the battle
must have been bloody, but as often as not, thanks to the
three horns and the protective shield of bone, Triceratops
would have been the victorious survivor.

Pronounciation. Try-SERR-uh-tops
Name. 'Three-horned face'
Type. Ceratopsid
Period. Upper Cretaceous (70 million
 years ago)
Measurements. Over 6 metres (20 feet)
 long, weighed 7–8 tons
Food. Plants
Where found. North America

Tyrannosaurus

Tyrannosaurus means 'tyrant lizard' and Tyrannosaurus often has the word Rex, meaning 'King', added to its name. It certainly was a king among dinosaurs and a tyrant too. It was a huge, fierce meat-eater, who walked on enormous hind feet and had long, sharp claws on its three large toes. It had a massive jaw, filled with huge, thick, sabre-like teeth. Some of the teeth were six inches long and it used them to tear the flesh off its prey. It didn't then use them to chew the meat: almost certainly, it swallowed it whole.

To keep up its strength and to feed its vast body, Tyrannosaurus had to spend almost all its time hunting. It was the largest and the strongest of all the meat-eating dinosaurs, and on dry land there were few creatures that could hope to come out of a fight with it alive, though Triceratops was one.

(It should be noted that while most scientists agree that Tyrannosaurus was a savage killer who hunted its prey, there are some scientists who believe that its body was too big and too bulky to enable it to chase other creatures and that it only fed off the bodies of *dead* animals.)

Pronounciation. Teh-ran-oh-SAW-russ
Name. 'Tyrant lizard'
Type. Carnosaur
Period. Upper Cretaceous (70 million years ago)
Measurements. 13 metres (42 feet) long, 5 metres (16 feet) high, weighed 8 tons
Food. Meat
Where found. North America, eastern Asia

Fun With Dinosaurs

Where To See Dinosaurs

Since they disappeared seventy million years ago, there is nowhere where you can see real live dinosaurs today. However, there are a number of museums throughout the United Kingdom where you can see fossilised remains of dinosaurs, and several where you can see reconstructed models of dinosaurs. In London, at the British Museum of Natural History in Cromwell Road, you will find some impressive dinosaur skeletons and a series of fascinating paintings and models showing dinosaurs in their natural surroundings. Also in London, at the Crystal Palace Park, you can see some life-size reconstructions of prehistoric animals. They were made over a hundred years ago and are not accurate in their detail, but they are interesting to look at nonetheless.

You will be able to find out at your local library where the nearest collection of prehistoric animals and fossils can be found, but museums in each of the following British towns are known for their good displays of prehistoric exhibits:

Belfast, Birmingham, Bristol, Cardiff, Edinburgh, Liverpool, Lyme Regis, Manchester, Newcastle-upon-Tyne, Oxford, Sandown, Isle of Wight, Sheffield.

Where to read about Dinosaurs

If you would like to learn more about dinosaurs, you might like to read one or more of these useful and interesting books:

COLLINS BOOKS OF DINOSAURS by Tom McGowen (published by *Collins*)

DINOSAURS AND OTHER PREHISTORIC ANIMALS by Alfred Leutscher (*Hamlyn*)

THE DINOSAURS by W. E. Swinton (*British Museum*)

FOSSIL AMPHIBIANS AND REPTILES by W. E. Swinton (*British Museum*)

FOSSILS by F. H. T. Rhodes and H. S. Zim (*Hamlyn*)

FUN WITH PALAEONTOLOGY by William C. Cartner (*Kaye & Ward*)

LIFE BEFORE MAN by Z. W. Spinar (*Thames & Hudson*)

THE LIFE OF PREHISTORIC ANIMALS by W. R. Hamilton (*Macdonald*)

THE WONDERFUL WORLD OF PREHISTORIC ANIMALS by W. E. Stanton (*Macdonald*)

Draw a Dinosaur

If you want to know how to draw a Styracosaurus, follow these simple instructions.

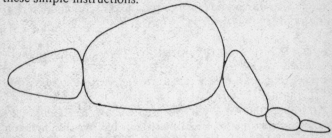

1. Draw a pencil outline for the body and head of Styracosaurus, with three ovals for his tail.

2. Add the legs, making three ovals to each leg, connected where the joints would be.

3. Draw a complete outline around the pencil circles to give a definite shape to the dinosaur.

4. Add long spikes to his head.

5. Shape his face and draw a horn above his snout. Add pointed toes to his feet.

6. Rub out the pencil circles.

7. Draw his mouth, eye, and nostril and continue the bottom of the spikes under his eye.

8. Add the folds and wrinkles of his skin.

9 Finally colour your dinosaur a dappled light brown. Give his skin plenty of warts.

Make a Model Dinosaur

To make a handsome model of Diplodocus this is what
you will need:

> A plastic bottle
> Some stiff wire
> Some old newspaper
> Two large, flimsy polythene bags
> (dry cleaners' bags are ideal)
> Paint
> Glue
> Sellotape
> Scissors
> Wire-cutters
> Paintbrushes

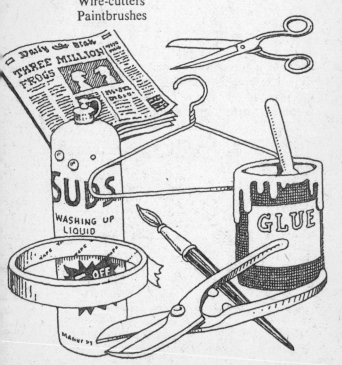

And this is what you do:

1. Cut two pieces of wire – wire from a coat-hanger will do – and bend them round the top and the bottom of the bottle to act as Diplodocus's legs. Sellotape the wire to the bottle and shape the legs.

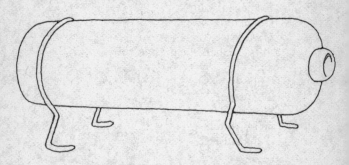

2. Cut another piece of wire, this time a much longer one, and run it through the length of the bottle. This wire should extend at the front to act as the neck and at the back to act as the tail. Sellotape the wire to the bottle and shape it into position.

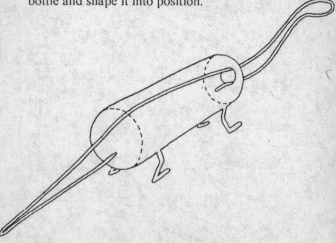

. Now cut up fairly large pieces of newspaper and roll them round the bottle and the wire to give some 'body' to Diplodocus. It doesn't matter if the newspaper gets crumpled. You will need to put lots on his neck and tail and legs. Each layer of newspaper should be Sellotaped into position and you should shape the newspaper so that the neck and tail really look like Diplodocus's neck and tail.

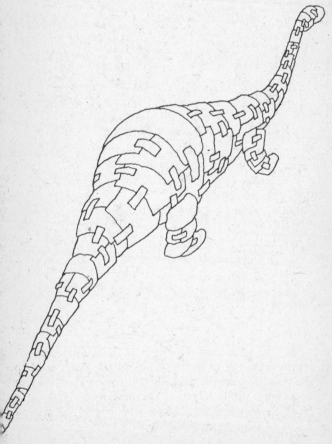

4. Take one of the polythene bags and spread glue all over the inside of it. Now place the polythene bag over the head of Diplodocus and wrap it round his body and forelegs as far back as the bag will stretch. Try to smooth the bag as best you can, but don't worry if the bag gets wrinkled. Diplodocus is supposed to have wrinkled skin.

5. Spread glue all over the inside of the second polythene bag and pull it over Diplodocus's tail. Stretch it over his tail, his hind legs and his body and glue this second bag down firmly where it overlaps with the first bag. Now cover the whole model with a coat of glue and leave it to dry overnight.

6. When the model is dry you can paint it – and you can paint it any colour or colours you like because nobody knows the colour of the original Diplodocus. And when you are painting him, don't forget to give him a good face, with a happy grin and sparkling eyes!

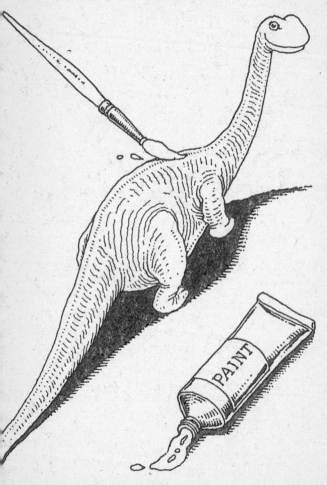

Make a Monster Dinosaur

To make a huge model of a terrifying Tyrannosaurus Rex this is what you will need:

> 2.5 metres of wire
> Some old newspaper
> Paint
> Glue paste made from flour and water
> Sellotape
> Some thin cardboard
> Scissors
> Wire-cutters
> Paintbrushes

And this is what you do:

1. Take a piece of wire about 83 cm long and shape it into the head and backbone. Twist the wire together at the neck.

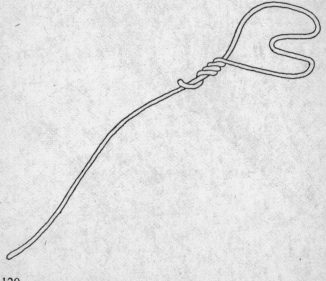

2. Attach another piece of wire about 50 cm long to form the underside of the dinosaur.

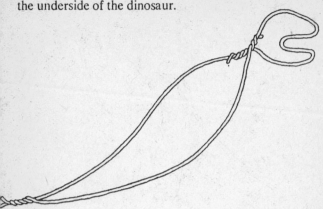

3. Take 55 cm of wire and shape it into the outline of a leg. Make it wide at the top and thin at the foot. Make a second leg in the same way. Join the back part of the legs together at the top.

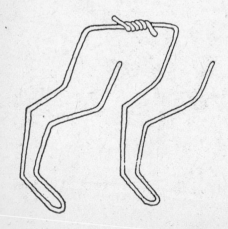

4. Join the loose ends of the legs to the backbone.

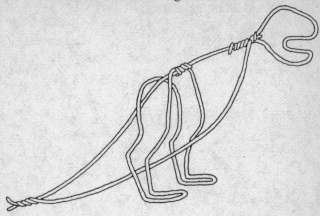

5. The arms are made from 20 cm of wire bent into a U
   shape. Attach it to the spine as shown. The frame i
   now complete; adjust it so that it stands properly.

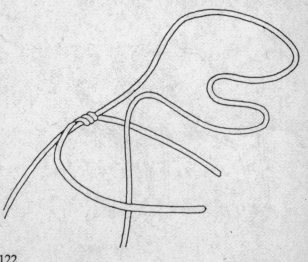

Now roll up lots and lots of sheets of newspaper so that they form thin tubes. Roll these thin tubes of newspaper around the dinosaur's wire frame and Sellotape each tube into position.

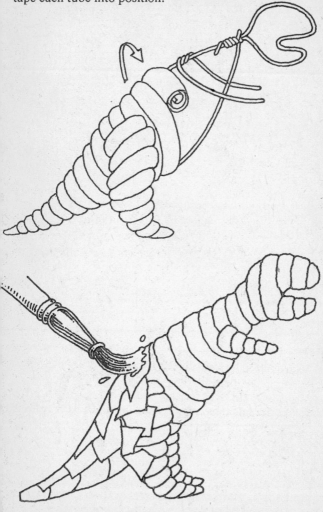

7. Tear some more newspaper into pieces about 5 cm by 5 cm. Soak the paper in glue made from flour and water then paste the model over with the paper. Cover every part of Tyrannosaurus and put on several layers.

8. Out of the thin cardboard cut sharp-toes for Tyrannosaurus's feet, claws for his hands and vast teeth for his jaws. Glue them all into position. When the glue has dried completely, you can paint your mighty Tyrannosaurus – and then stand him in the window so he frightens the neighbours!

Prehistoric Crossword

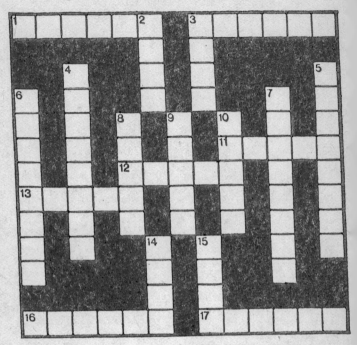

Clues Across

1. Ankylosaurus was protected by this. His was made of bone. Medieval knights were protected by it too, but theirs was made of metal.

3. The technical name for the remains of past life preserved in stone or rock.

11. The technical name for a creature that walks on two legs.

12. To a peaceful plant-eater like Anatosaurus, Tyrannosaurus was a deadly - - - - -.

13. Tyrannosaurus was certainly one of these, only he was never as gentle as the one Beauty fell in love with in · the fairy story.

16. The Greek for this word is 'sauros'.

17. If a dinosaur was a reptile, what is a human being?

Clues Down

2. The substance in which you would expect to find a fossil preserved.
3. The number of feet on which Brachiosaurus, Brontosaurus and Diplodocus used to walk.
4. The name of this extinct reptile means 'terrible lizard'.
5. Ornithischia is the technical name for describing a group of dinosaurs whose hip bones were formed in a certain way. How are Ornithischia described in English?
6. Hadrosaurs were a group of dinosaurs easily recognised by the unusual shapes of their jaws. Anatosaurus was a famous Hadrosaur. How would you describe his jaw in English?
7. This is what dinosaurs, crocodiles, turtles and lizards all are.

8. They were fifteen centimetres long and as sharp as daggers, and you found them in the jaws of Tyrannosaurus Rex. What were they?
9. Lambeosaurus had one of these on top of his head shaped like a strange hatchet. Corythosaurus had one shaped like a half circle. What was it?
10. Word for a deep gorge or chasm and if you (or a dinosaur) fell down one you would be lost forever.
14. Ornitholestes got his name from two Greek words. 'Lestes' means 'stealer'. What does 'ornitho' mean?
15. Dinosaurs were cold-blooded creatures, so what kind of climate did they need?

(You will find the solution to the crossword on page 128)

Solution to the prehistoric crossword.

Across: 1. Armour 3. Fossil 11. Biped 12. Enemy
13. Beast 16. Lizard 17. Mammal
Down: 2. Rock 3. Four 4. Dinosaur 5. Birdhips
6. Duckbill 7. Reptiles 8. Teeth 9. Crest 10. Abyss
14. Bird 15. Warm